Stare of Pigmentation
A Chapbook

Indigo Green

THE
OCEAN DEEP

Stare of Pigmentation: A Chapbook by Indigo Green

Copyright © 2022 Indigo Green

For permissions contact: TCsJournall@gmail.com

Cover by Indigo Green

Illustrated by Chloe Smalls Johnson & Careese Collier-Price

ISBN: 978-1-957674-01-8 (print)

ISBN: 978-1-957674-07-0 (digital)

Published by The Ocean Deep Publishing

13833 Dumfries Rd, Manassas, VA 20112

Printed in USA

First edition 2022

*To the lives lost, harmed, trumatized, and negatively
effected by the history of brutality
towards people of color in America.
For the party people of room 1313.*

Table of Contents

SECTION 1: CLOSED LIDS

SECTION 2: SQUINTING

SECTION 3: STARE

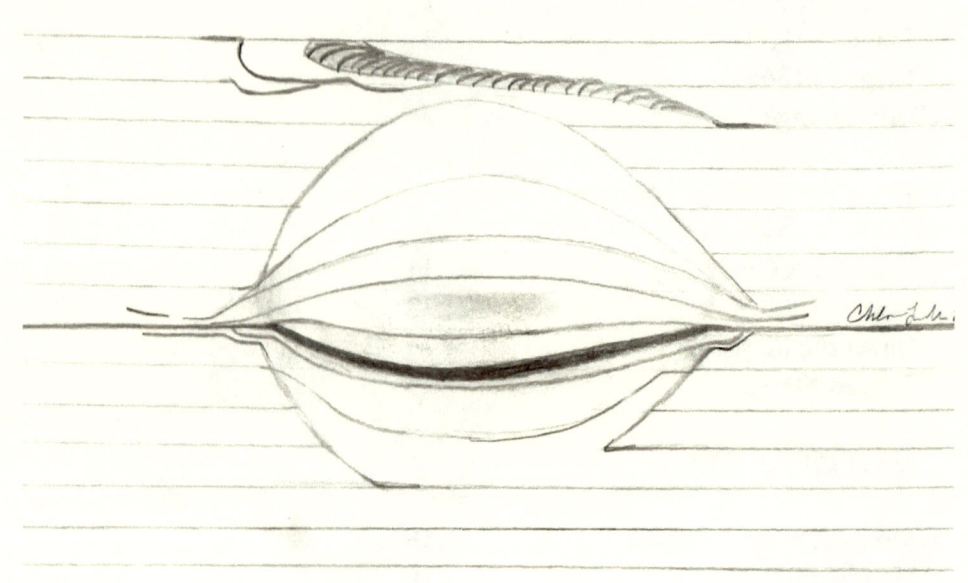

False Prophets

A nation's descent is forming a secure platform to hold a man higher
than he thinks of himself.
You hammer the nail, mounting this figure above your morals.

Logic is a shared occurrence. Original thought begets original thought,
And through the process is analyzed or accepted as a fact.

But in that process, if the only people in the validation room mirror in
mindedness,
A reason to amend or reform a proposed notion- never uttered out the
mouth.

Did the Socratic trio watch the sky while they created the stars?
Did they pull up the sun and push down the moon?

Did they draw the equator and force blacks below
So when the earth shifts around the sun, only melanin grows.

After all this is done—deities among bodies.
Bodies with no control according to concocted theory.

Where sunbeams its highest heat and rain is rarely recurring
Where grounds of sand and mines of gold cultivate beauty

Even where the word culture was curated
And our rock- the birthplace of creation itself

That same land? Inhabited by burnt faces-
Burnt with no intellect, no self-government?

Were they burnt with inferiority?
Or just browned with such beauty?

Blessed with brawn and behavior to battle
The beatings of benevolent-deficient bitches.

Protective and polished with prowess to pan the petulant pandemics
perspiring on pride lands

To the supposed deities drenched in jealously, that shortens the Nile
You probably **smile** with joy knowing your scripture makes justice a joke.

Tagged #1833

Number 1833 laid upon the chest (so far from the

neck) still grasps the trachea behind the flesh
And stays burnished in a sandy ebony
Like the ash upon the knee
Or also in the cracked plain between the thumb and index

Each imprinted foot track made by this disheveled man
With a dowry soul (the transaction between torment and his flesh)
Cements the only path allowed to hold the pace of steps
Between the horrid plantation and the looming temptation of the shops

They once sold souls on shelves along with bottles of children's or
mother's tears collected after the uttered words
"Sold to the man-"
Now only apples reach the counter for cash

Tagged #1865

My child,

Wade in the water to remove our scent. Keep from the tilled land with sown crops.
Cleanse from their snowy white tops, deceivingly plush at its end,
But hidden is a thorn poisoned with a plague of imprisonment.

And if nicked, this scent will linger for life.

And yes,

Your knees can sore while pleading to inhale the atmosphere where exoneration is abundant,
But I myself was impaled. Now chains, whether forged and fabricated for your mind or wrists, become a dominant gene in our bloodline.

I apologize.

I drench in deep remorse, sponging each tear flowing from your eyes.
In my ascension, I hope I leave you in a world without the blood I paid
Each time I was picked by a cotton tip or each limb I swelled in manual labor.

My child,

Tell me about your life. Tell me of your dreams. I don't want to hear my curse has now left me.
Tell me your hopes and what you desire. Devotion and desire should be all that you tire.

In the days you walk the earth, I hope you see- life instead of the pain strung upon me.

Dear momma,

There was nowhere to wade, so I washed in my tears. I bathed in the blood
from cotton spheres
I don't blame myself cause you said I could see-- damage-- or chains forged
just for me.
The blacksmith inscribed numbers 1-8-6-5,
but I could feel it, burned to my skin.

And yes,

I sadly sunk in sorrow and sponged it in my spine.
I stand straight, so straight I make strain seem fine.
And stemmed from my stature is me steeping in stains
From shoveling the same grounds holding your origins of pain.

In forgiveness,

My heart swells with a strenuous appreciation. For you carry so much for me,
forgetting your shoulders have the load of the world to bear.
You had to (carry) fund this earth; every crop should hold your name,
And you should be the only founding face on a bill.

Dear Momma,

I thought thirteen was a lucky number when it graced the page of the
constitution
But the word loophole is the most honest word in the book.
It drags you down a spiral and as you plunge
You can finally see how vague law really is. How easily we can be brutalized
from an ink stroke.

And lastly,

In my one day of memory, peace takes hold of me

A disheveled homeless man sits as far as I can see

When I open my eyes, what lies awaiting me

That same man handing me a tool for (my) loitering and (his) vagrancy

And if I ever leave these gates, my mind would gain the ability

To realize a dog is treated better than me.

I Am Strange Fruit

Disguised in the nighttime by the cloak of the woods
Castrated by the bedsheets tainted with juice from my strange fruit
Thick as the cracks in my ancestors' backs

With age, those torn muscles are more like beauty scars than painful shards
of broken glass cutting within the skin

In the hour, my juice turns sour and fertilizes the ground
After I lose my breath and dark-chafing purple rug burn on my neck

Let the chill winds carry my soul home

Tomorrow, for my next of kin with radicalized coils creepin' out their scalp
Fighting for the voice I've wanted to shed to my people
But I was silenced by this life I never chose

This die quiet, say quiet, don't look the wrong way or direction world we're
born into
Where my children could soon join me in this unmarked graveyard of slave
last names

I am strange fruit. The cop cars cargo
If I'm lucky
Ship me off to a foreign land
Where I'll rarely see a man
The color of the inside of my hand that's been dipped in tan

And If I'm not, take your best shot and leave me to bleed in the same street
Where my legends marched in footsteps to fight for the air in my lungs
To continue to circulate throughout my body
Helping me live through each breath I take

Talking to heaven in rewinding time
Before lying in my juice

I remind myself of this occurrence
How'd get in this place?
Hopefully soon you'll get to see my face
                                    To be televised (TBT)

Here he comes with sirens. Lights flash in my rear. I slow down, pull over, try
to encase my fear
My hand trembles while I reach for my papers
And place them up on my dash
Take my keys out the ignition and they follow with shake

*Keep your hands in sight- only say yes or no cause you gotta be there to watch ya
garden grow*
Footsteps get closer I hear a crunch on the ground
Try not to flinch and throw ya body around
Don't make sudden movements- keep your hands in
You don't wanna be lined up in the aim of gunsight
License and registration travels to my ear
Those might be the last words I ever get to hear

For a moment I caught a glimpse of the officer's robin egg eyes, I remember
more than his name Or badge number
And maybe I should have glanced away
But when his pupils dilated he turned off the safety

I knew you can't breathe as a victim of a knee
But you lose your breath knowing those eyes can be your separation between
life or death

To my second kin
I hope ya blood doesn't boil with too much rage
But instead boils like water for tea
Rages like that fire with a peaceful transition
And the result is as sweet as honey and peach
So you're no longer strange fruit, not yet ripe to eat
But strong fruit with a presence that overtakes defeat

Let the seeds I've planted in you sprout so far
That you become the tree that bears
That nectar of knowledge we need
To combat the destructive-choppers of trees

"Get on your knees!" "Stay on the ground!"

Slammed on the car; *man I'm already down!*
You profit off our pain but
you'll never see
the gardens
we've planted
while you focus on me.

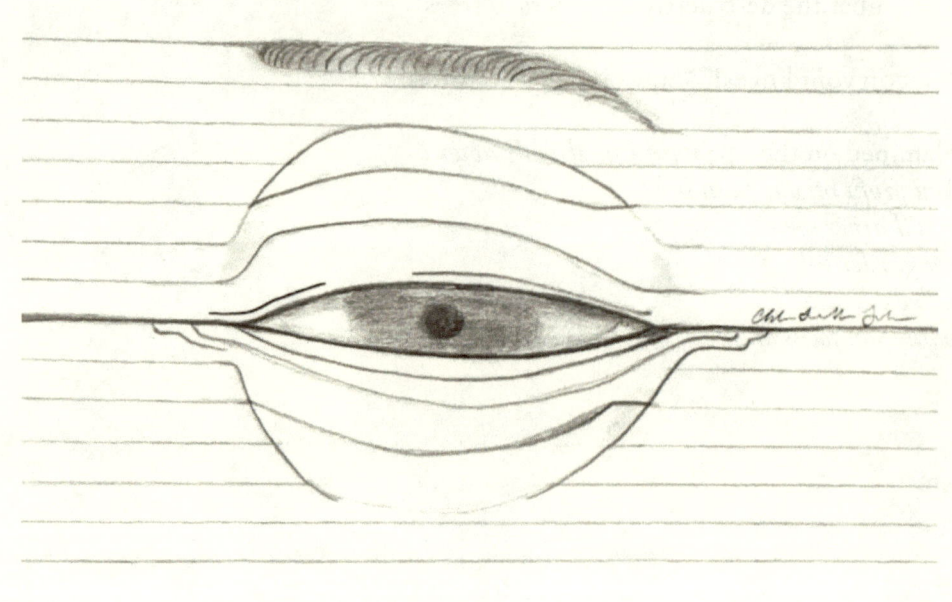

Grandma's Chair

You can see the stars burn tonight
And cricket stridulation twists your intestines
As you venture through the red sea parted to paneled porch steps.

Dark brushed douglas fir panels the decked floor with gaps dat you can fit a thumb in
And the porch-
Home for the hand-carved rocking chairs where rivers flow downstream
And intersect in inconclusiveness-

The streams would leave themselves imprinted on your back, arms, and hands
Seeping its advisory in your docile skin.

Though weathered, the other chair still leaves its mark—or more significantly—
A splinter in your back—
That viciously stern deception. A blessing perception at first, but you fall short in anticipating impaling
A lifetime supply at that—it stings bad.

Like gracing your hand along freshly molded nails
And the grand old carving is more like branding.

My scar for life.

Dogtags

Left. Left. Left, right, left.
We. Have. Nothing left.

Mommas are home, and babies are born
While I'm out at sea, my family is torn.
My brothers are dyin'.
My sisters are cryin'.
And I'm tryin' to stay alive

Left. Left. Left, right, left.
I. Have. Nothing left.
My soldiers are dyin'.
Their families are cryin', and young fathers are lyin'-
With fertile field

Thank God for the baby- Army, and Navy
Cause' yall'd call me crazy if I'd leave.
As I return home from my ships in the sea
And finally arrived at the place that birthed me
I'm met with the hate- same established at war; I-

I thought that some peace would be left for me.
But I hold America's pains.
And now when I see
my son's body for me
To lay rest inside his grave.

A funeral home now holds his name
And the military is all I can blame
If I returned home from my ships in the sea
The blood would be mine
Not his over me

So now when I see
my son's body for me
To lay rest in his homicide grave
I'll love God for the Navy

America's
Baby
for driving
me crazy
for life.

Left. Left. Left, right, left.
I. Am. Nothing. Left.

Dawn the Masquerade

FOR I SEE ALL!
Bending binary for ya truth—I SEE Y'ALL!

You old queens and new children
Buoyant and GAYzing upon the stage
As I hoist my authentic voice out from the depths of my vocal cords
NO MORE STREP FA ME HONEY!
        I'M NOT QUIET, I DON'T SILENCE!
                HAHA!

And all is good!

It could be. Silent. And dark as day outside
But the night shines here
Where the dark is an ally-we step steppin' in heels
And not stumblin' in oxfords or timbs

And when a buttoned-down makes an uplifted gown,   WOO!

I HOPE NO BRICKS FLY TODAY!

I HOPE NO-

I-

Tagged #1982

1982 through 84'
I got Mr. Coke knockin' down my door
Nah, not the type I saw Scarface get
My joint is freebased nd dis shit is lit

5 to 15 nd I'm already gone
Damn euphoria should be labeled a con
I'm selling all the clothes off my back
It's too late now I'm addicted to crack!

1982 through 84'
I'm Mr.Coke bustin' down ya door
You could be Nancy Reagan nd jus say no
Buh da green in ya pocket makes my loot grow

I got people comin' from everywhere
You could try to lock me down, buh I just don't care
Cause when you hand me dat 20, nd I give you a rock
I'll see you a lul later runnin' to my block

1982, 3,4, nd 5
Happy I'm still breathin' nd happy ta be alive
It's me, Mr. D holdin' down my blocks
Nd everybody nd dey momma posted up wit Glocks

Show no emotion nd show no fear
Any sign of weakness nd you out da clear
Nowhere ta hide, get caught outside
Now you nd lul Timmy can spell drive-by

1982, 3, 4, 5, 6
I'm still Mr. D with my bag of tricks
Remember lul Timmy 82' through 5
His lul friend Nicky jus learned ta fly

Nicky got caught by a loaded clip
It was jus cocked back, aimed up, nd zip
It's just another day, a lul homicide
I'll see you kids on sunday witcha suit nd tie

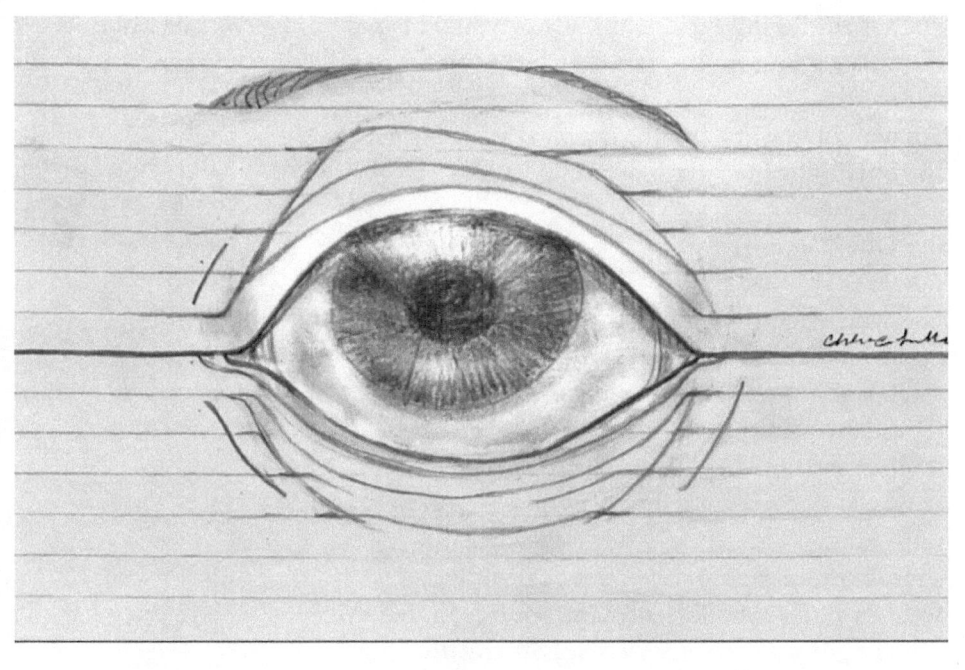

Momma Sang the Blues

And she said, "Oh how the world ain't ready for ya."

"Moonlight shines in midnight suppressing the intensity of daylight, and
when it shines in ya room, just know you'll be aight cause' we talk about stars
illuminating our nights, but they burn too far to tell you ya bright."

But here in my city, it's like the world never sleeps
The only light I receive is artificial LEDs-

She said, "Trees grow tall, the tops you'll never see-"

And Ma, when they touch the sky, they're only avoiding me
Cause I ain't ever gonna fly, I don't ever get to soar
You left too soon; I'm left unassured
I could grow in this world with no image of you

sacrificed ya life   for ya child   you never knew

Those hospital doors slide open real wide
but they'll never match the width of my dilated eyes
When I got notified you were leavin' my life.
Damn, I wish my dad took better care of his wife.

And maybe I'm jus using him as a source to hold blame
And maybe I do that to project all my pain
Cause' I was ready to meet my mom. I squirmed to see her face.
I might notta smiled yet, but there would be one in its place
Till' I could feel her heartbeat, and it was slower than mine
So I sped mine up hopin' she'd match its time
My heart accelerates, buh I feel hers
                                          drop
As mine keeps **PU** mp **IN'**   I feel hers stop.

Now I wonder If my palpitations ended ya life
Like my oblivion made you bleed out,   out of my life.
You gave all your nutrients in turn to nurture me
And your eyes started closing before you could even see
Me take-

3/5   a loving sacrifice

                                                    Chrees Collier-price

Handprints

I would rather you brush your hand across my chest
Or slap my face than simply place
Your hand on my shoulder

That's not obvious enough. The responsibility of exposure is a taxing event
I would be willing to partake in
but I've been

Molded into a silhouette of opinions and expectations.
Primed and painted over. Subjugated by another's wishes
Forced to let myself dry.

I miss the ignorance;
My juvenile innocence where I painted with my hands, and feet
Where no painting in my world had to be neat

I would get some on me and no one would care
Until my difference in shades remained there.

I would rather you soak me in solvents
Than lock your hand around my forearm permitting slight exposure
Cause' I can handle that expense I have to pay

Every time I walk out my door there's a possibility I won't come back
Signed on my canvas
Young. Trans. Black.

Static, No Shock
It's not even graceful-
Usually, tears are free-flowing- continuously grazing down pores
But they still reach their end

And usually, the eyes are a fiery rose.
engulfing the pupil in reddish-orange flames
And the leftover tears congregate on the precipice of your eyelid
Just glossing the cornea.

And usually-usually there's breath breaking itself through my lips
Trying to remind me I'm still alive
I can continue to live.

But my body standing there stiff and almost fragile
like a winter branch trying to last until spring
Straining my eyes fixing on this body under someone's patella-
Laying still above an MSNBC headline

Usually, tears are free-flowing
But I had no grace, no fiery rose
And if I did have tears,

It's the hallucinatory black and white static of-
Truth- never televised.

Indigo Green is a graduate of Colgan High School's Creative Writing program in 2022. He is currently studying sociology in undergraduate school at George Mason University.

Indigo has a passion for illuminating the truths and wonders of humanity. He doesn't hesitate to discuss topics evocatively. His authenticity provides insight and perspective from many facets of life, allowing any reader to immerse in something new or reflect on something old.

Indigo participated in the 2022 prince William county NAACP Inaugural Competition, winning first place in the written poetry category.

He plays guitar and collects vinyl, CDs, and vintage magazines in his free time. You can view his works like "Momma Sang Da Blues" in Siren Literary Journal.